Plants on My Plate

Cathy Smith

I am eating the seeds of a plant.
These seeds are peas.

They are from a pea plant.

seeds

I am eating the leaves of a plant.
These leaves are spinach.

They are from a spinach plant.

leaves

I am eating the stems of a plant.
These stems are celery.

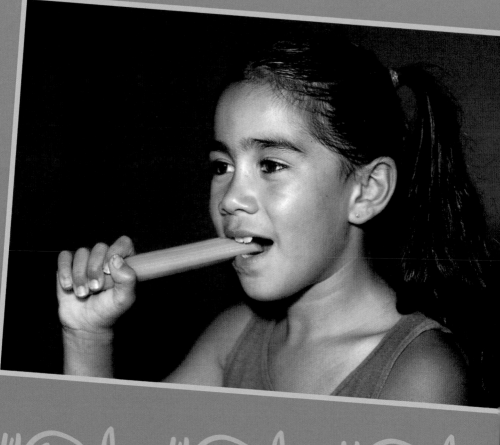

They are from a celery plant.

stems

7

I am eating the roots of a plant.
These roots are carrots.

They are from a carrot plant.

roots

9

I am eating the flower buds of a plant.
These flower buds are broccoli.

They are from a broccoli plant.

flower buds

What part of a plant will you eat today?

Index